WATERLOO LOCAL SCHOOL
MIDDLE SCHOOL LIBRARY

796.
325
ath

power volleyball

Consultant

Jim Coleman, professor
George Williams College
Downers Grove, Illinois
Coach, U.S. Volleyball Team
1968 Olympic Games

Demonstrators

Smitty Duke
Jack Henn
Mary Jo Peppler
Mary Perry
Al Scates
Rudy Suwara
Jane Ward

published by:
The Athletic Institute
Merchandise Mart, Chicago

A not-for-profit organization devoted to the advancement of athletics, physical education and recreation.

© The Athletic Institute 1972
All Rights Reserved
Reprinted 1975

**Library of Congress
Catalog Card Number 79-109498**

**"Sports Techniques" Series
SBN 87670-038-5**

Published by The Athletic Institute
Chicago, Illinois 60654

Foreword

The **"Sports Techniques" Series** is a comprehensive set of instructional aids in sports which are made available by The Athletic Institute. This book is part of a master plan which seeks to make the benefits of athletics, physical education and recreation available to everyone.

The Athletic Institute, a not-for-profit organization devoted to the advancement of athletics, physical education and recreation, believes that sports participation by young and old has benefits of inestimable value to the individual.

The nature and scope of the many Institute programs are determined by nationally-known professional educators who are noted for their outstanding knowledge and expertise in their fields.

The Institute believes that through this book the reader will become more proficient and skilled in the fundamentals of this fine sport. Knowledge and the practice necessary to mold knowledge into playing ability are the keys to real enjoyment in playing any game or sport.

Donald E. Bushore
Executive Director
The Athletic Institute

Introduction

Volleyball is one of the world's most popular sports. The sport is played in over 80 countries, some 25 of which recognize the game as a major sport.

Volleyball became a part of the Olympics in 1964, and since then the growth of the sport in the United States has been phenomenal. Volleyball is becoming increasingly popular throughout our nation's schools and colleges.

Power volleyball is distinguished from recreational volleyball by the amount of organization needed for a highly refined implementation of team strategy and individual skills. Power volleyball is a game for players who possess a certain amount of quickness, alertness, coordination and stamina, and who desire to further develop the same. All of the foregoing qualities are essential to the mastery of the game's complex skills and game situations.

Six fundamentals important to power volleyball play are presented within this book. Playing techniques have changed with the passing years and continue to change. Therefore, only the most basic fundamentals and techniques fall within the scope of this book.

Please note the descriptions are made relative to a right-handed player and should be mirrored by a left-handed player.

Jim Coleman

Table of Contents

the serve
    Ready Position 7
    Striking Techniques 8
        Point of Contact 10
        Follow Through 11

the forearm pass
    Forearm Pass Techniques 13
        Arm Action 14
        Contact 15

the set
    Set Techniques 17
        Ready Position 17
        Preparing to Set 18
        Ball Contact 18
        Body Motion and Follow Through ... 19

the spike
    Spiking Techniques 22
        Two-Foot Takeoff 22
        Arm Action 24
        Ball Contact 25
        Follow Through 26

the block
    The Defensive Block 28
    The Offensive Block 30

the Japanese roll
    Japanese Roll Techniques 33

rules simplified
    Diagram of Court 35
    The Court 36
    Equipment 36
    The Game 37
    Team Tactics 38

glossary of power volleyball terms 45

the serve

The effective volleyball serve is a combination of power, accuracy and action. Techniques and tactics for the serve vary greatly from player to player and are probably the most individualistic part of the game.

The serve most commonly used in competition is the *floater,* a serve which puts minimal spin on the ball. This serve is similar to the "knuckleball" pitch in baseball in that the action of the ball is unpredictable. The ball will rise, drop or slide. The floating action does not depend upon maximum power, so it may be quite effective for younger, smaller or weaker players. It can be easily taught and even inexperienced players can quickly learn to place this serve accurately into the opponent's court. Studies have shown that over a wide spectrum of competition the team with the most effective servers will win approximately three out of every four games.

Ready Position

The serve is initiated from a ready position while standing safely behind the end line (white) of the court. Feet should be comfortably spread and ready to stride forward. The ball is held in both hands. Concentration on the ball and on the serving target while in the ready position helps determine the degree of success of the serve.

1. STAND BEHIND END LINE OF COURT IN READY POSITION.

2. SPREAD FEET COMFORTABLY APART. HOLD BALL IN BOTH HANDS. CONCENTRATE ON BALL AND TARGET.

Striking Techniques

From the ready position toss the ball gently into the air with the nonhitting hand. Shift weight by striding forward with the foot opposite the hitting hand. The hitting arm is drawn back and cocked. Concentrate on the ball.

The cocked arm position is somewhat similar to that of a football quarterback who is attempting to pass. The forward arm swing is a symmetrical, rhythmic movement. As the striking arm moves forward, the opposite arm moves backward as a counterbalance.

While moving toward the ball which is now coming straight down, the forward arm swing is led by the elbow of the striking arm. Note the symmetrical body rotation around the vertical axis. The final arm action before contact with the ball is a rapid snap of the upper arm from the elbow.

For accurate serving, the ball must be placed consistently in the same position for each serve. It is

3. GENTLY TOSS BALL IN AIR WITH NONSTRIKING HAND.
4. STRIDE FORWARD WITH LEG OPPOSITE HITTING HAND.

5. LEAD FORWARD SWING OF ARM WITH ELBOW.

6. ROTATE BODY SLIGHTLY.

only in this manner that one can hope to master the serve. Normally the ball will be slightly in front of the body and high enough for full arm extension.

Maximum concentration should be focused upon the ball the instant before contact. At contact the body should be in balance.

7. CONTINUE ARM ACTION FORWARD AND CONTACT BALL WITH A STRONG "SNAPPING" MOTION.

8. COMPLETE SWING WITH FOLLOW THROUGH.

Point of Contact

Contact with the ball must be solid. The striking force must be applied through the center of the ball to eliminate spin.

The striking surface for most servers is the heel of the open hand with the rest of the hand applying some force to assure that the ball has minimal spin as it leaves the hand. It is important to note that some servers prefer not to use the open hand, full body extension or the same relationship of ball to body, yet they develop a very consistent serving pattern.

Contact the ball solidly to clear the net and descend upon the receiver rather quickly.

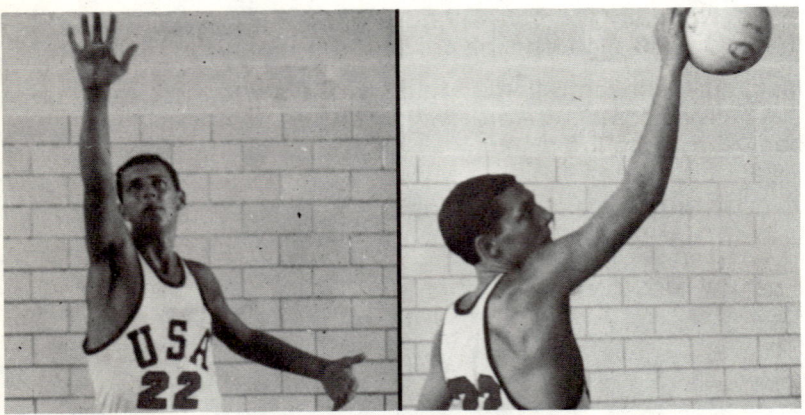

9. CONTACT BALL WITH HEEL OF OPEN HAND.

10. PUNCH BALL ON LOW TRAJECTORY OVER NET.

Follow Through

A smooth follow through is the sign of a well disciplined, consistent server. The techniques of serving are the same for both men and women.

It is generally believed that the serve is a much more effective weapon in the women's game because the lower net allows the ball to descend upon the receiver more quickly, thus making the pass more difficult to execute.

11. SMOOTH FOLLOW THROUGH AIDS CONSISTENCY.

Tip for Beginning Servers:

You may have better success by learning and practicing the underhand serve first.

Once this serve is mastered, you may choose to adopt the overhand method.

In situations where control is a prime factor, the underhand serve often is preferred.

the forearm pass

Until the mid-sixties, similar techniques were employed for both the *chest pass* and the *set*. Both passes were used to get the ball to the set man.

More recently, the *forearm pass* has found favor. While this particular pass sacrifices some accuracy, it affords greater court coverage and a higher percentage of success.

Forearm Pass Techniques

Feet should be comfortably spread with one foot slightly in front of the other. Ideally, the weight is on the balls of the feet, and the knees are flexed. The upper leg rises slightly from the horizontal so the angle formed at the knee is about 90 degrees.

The hands are clasped, usually one inserted in the palm of the other, and the thumbs are directed away from the body. Elbows are straight and close together with the arms rotated slightly outward to present a large flat area to contact the ball.

1. **FEET COMFORTABLY SPREAD APART, ONE FOOT SLIGHTLY AHEAD OF THE OTHER. WEIGHT ON BALLS OF FEET WITH KNEES FLEXED.**

2. **HANDS ARE CLASPED, ONE IN PALM OF THE OTHER. THUMBS POINT AWAY FROM BODY. ARMS ROTATED OUTWARD WITH ELBOWS STRAIGHT AND CLOSE TOGETHER.**

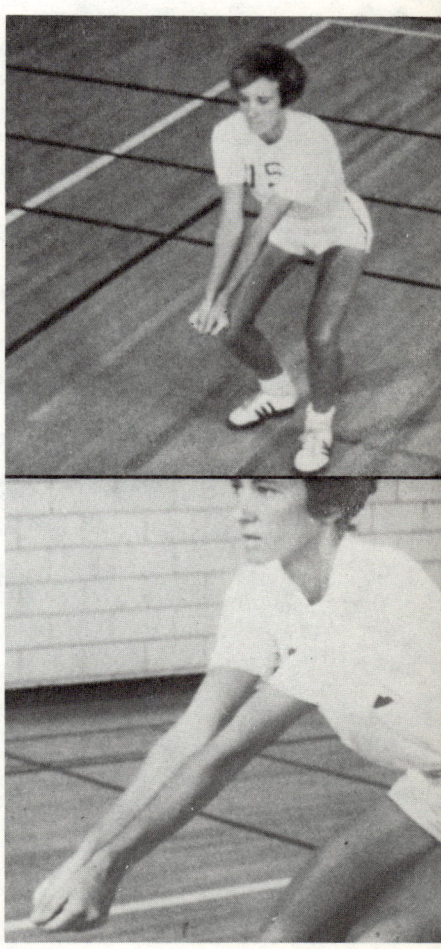

Arm Action

It is desirable to pass the ball from a relatively low height and directly in front of the body.

To contact the ball, swing the arms from the shoulders while "lifting" upward with the legs. The swing is not abrupt but is accomplished with finesse.

3. PLAY BALL IN FRONT OF BODY FROM RELATIVELY LOW HEIGHT.

4. SWING ARMS UPWARD WITH FINESSE.

Contact

Contact the ball above the wrists on the "soft" portion of arm. At the moment of contact, the angle at the shoulder should approximate 90 degrees between the upper arm and trunk. The arms are held horizontally and parallel to the upper leg.

Most importantly, keep eyes on the ball and follow through.

5. KEEP EYES ON BALL AND CONTACT BALL ABOVE WRISTS ON "SOFT" PORTION OF FOREARM.

   AT CONTACT, ARMS NEARLY HORIZONTAL AND PARALLEL WITH UPPER LEG.

6. FOLLOW THROUGH WITH EYES ON BALL.

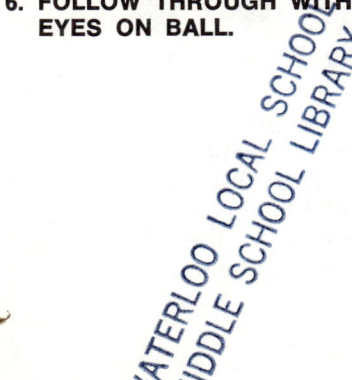

the set

The *set* or *face pass* is probably the most commonly taught and least understood of all the volleyball techniques. The difference between an effective and a "disastrous" offense is often the effectiveness of the set. The setter is really the quarterback of the volleyball team and upon his hands rides the success or failure of the team.

Set Techniques

Although the written rules insist that the ball cannot come to rest in a player's hands, that it cannot be carried and must be visibly hit, quite obviously such statements must be modified in light of the laws of physics and the interpretations of players, coaches and officials. In reality, often the ball which is smoothly caught and released is interpreted as being good and legal while the batted ball is penalized. Although there may be minor variations from player to player on a world-wide basis, virtually all successful setters use techniques similar to the ones presented here.

Ready Position

Assume a *ready position* about the time the ball begins its descent. In this position, the feet are comfortably spread with the body weight equally distributed on both feet. The knees are bent and ready to make minor position changes as the ball approaches. The heels should not carry much weight.

The wrists are cocked so that the angle between the forearm and the hand is 135 degrees or less.

Hands are cupped and relaxed. This relaxation is quite essential to smooth setting.

1. **FEET COMFORTABLY SPREAD WITH WEIGHT DISTRIBUTED EVENLY.**
2. **COCK WRISTS.**
3. **HANDS CUPPED AND RELAXED.**

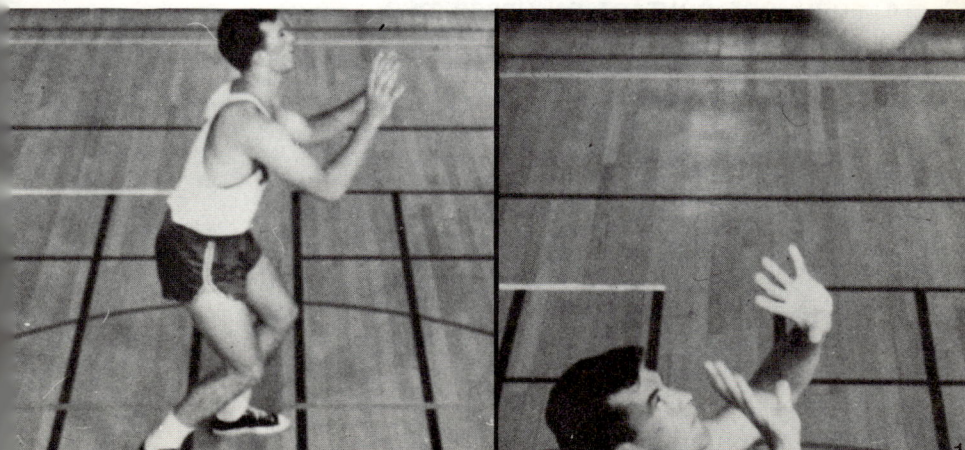

Preparing to Set

Normally, sight the ball through a "triangularly-shaped window" framed by the thumbs and index fingers. Caution should be observed in this position to see that the elbows are not spread too far outward. If the wrists are cocked, hands cupped and the triangle formed, the elbows should be in proper position.

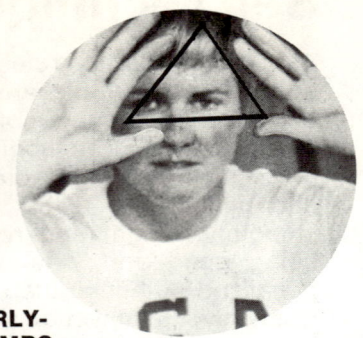

4. SIGHT BALL THROUGH TRIANGULARLY-SHAPED WINDOW FORMED BY THUMBS AND INDEX FINGERS.
   DO NOT SPREAD ELBOWS TOO FAR OUTWARD.

Ball Contact

Contact is made above the face or forehead on the appropriate contact points. The ball is definitely not batted, but actually remains in contact with the hands for an instant.

The major contact will come on the upper two sections of the index fingers. Somewhat less force is applied by the thumbs and middle fingers. Seldom will the outer two fingers on either hand contact the ball.

Most importantly, let the ball sink well into the hands.

5. CONTACT BALL ABOVE FACE OR FOREHEAD.
6. FOREMOST CONTACT ON UPPER TWO SECTIONS OF INDEX FINGERS. LESS FORCE APPLIED BY THUMBS AND MIDDLE FINGERS.

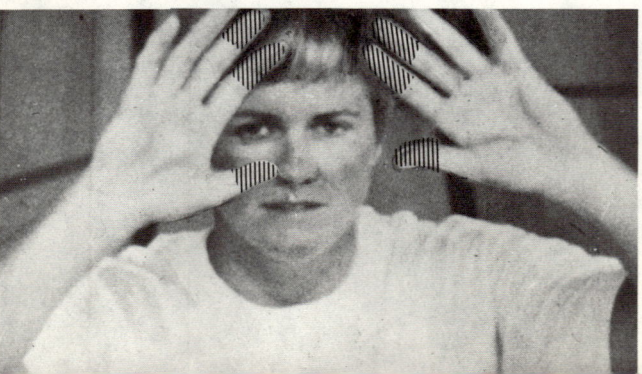

Body Motion and Follow Through

The major force applied to the ball is not that of wrist snap, but is more a coordinated body action through the ball. The line of force extends from the feet or trailing foot, through the center of gravity of the body and toward the ball. The follow through on the set does nothing to the ball, but serves to indicate a smooth, coordinated set. Neither the set nor the follow through should be a quick, jerky flick but instead should be a coordinated motion.

7. WATCH THE BALL ALL THE WAY INTO HANDS.

8. CONTACT BALL WITH "TRIANGLE" FORMED BY THUMBS AND INDEX FINGERS.

9. CONTACT MADE A FEW INCHES IN FRONT OF FACE OR FOREHEAD.

10. DO NOT BAT BALL AWAY, BUT LET BALL SINK DEEP WITHIN HANDS.

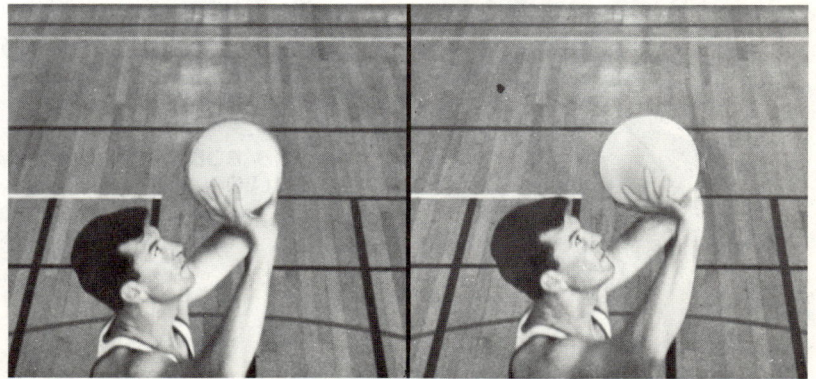

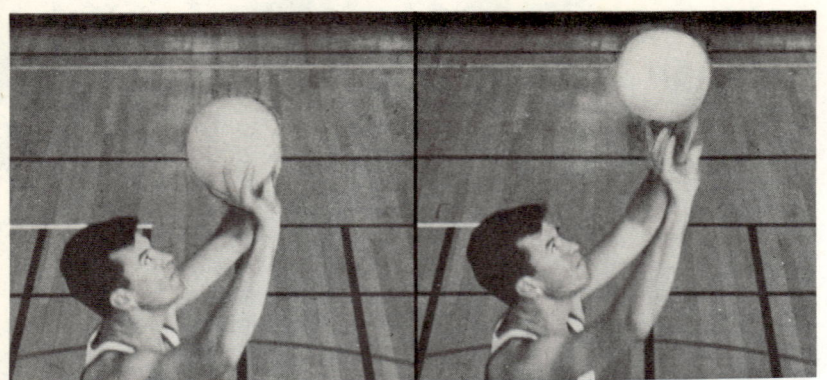

11. RAISE BODY AND HANDS THROUGH BALL.

12. EXTEND ARMS FULLY UPON RELEASE.

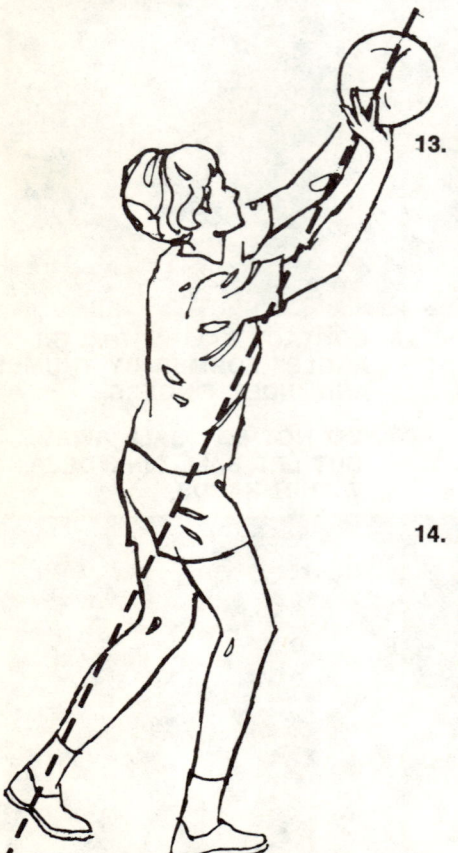

13. LINE OF FORCE EXTENDS FROM REAR LEG THROUGH CENTER OF GRAVITY TO DIRECTION OF BALL.

14. PROJECT BALL THROUGH COORDINATED BODY ACTION, NOT BY A SNAPPING ACTION OF WRISTS.

    EXTEND BODY MOTION UPWARD TO FOLLOW THROUGH.

the spike

The *spike* is the most dramatic part of the game of volleyball. Even though many studies have shown that it is one of the less important phases of the game, it is still a major attraction for both the spectator and the athlete.

The average well-spiked ball probably travels between 50 and 70 miles per hour.

Spiking Techniques

The action must begin with a good pass made to the setter. Normally, the spiker begins from 10 to 12 feet behind the net. Judge the trajectory of the set so as to contact the ball at the height of the jump. Mentally gauge the flight of the ball at the beginning of the approach. The normal approach is two or three steps.

Learn to attack from either the left or the right side of the court with little difference in technique. The *frontal approach* is usually preferred, whereby the spiker's angle to the net varies only slightly from a perpendicular line. This type of approach gives a better opportunity to observe the entire defense than does an approach from a wider angle.

1. ANGLE OF APPROACH VARIES ONLY SLIGHTLY FROM PERPENDICULAR LINE TO NET.
2. FRONTAL APPROACH AFFORDS OPPORTUNITY TO VIEW ENTIRE DEFENSE.

Two-Foot Takeoff

To achieve better body control while in the air, most spikers prefer to *take off* with both feet.

For greater height, drive the arms up forcefully from an extended position behind to straight overhead. The upward pull of the arms provides for a higher jump and position to cock the arm before swinging at the ball.

3. TWO-FOOT TAKEOFF AFFORDS BETTER BODY CONTROL. KEEP CENTER OF GRAVITY WELL BEHIND POINT OF CONTACT WITH FLOOR. EXTEND ARMS BEHIND BODY AND BEND KNEES DEEPLY. PLANT HEELS FIRMLY ON FLOOR FOR GOOD "HEEL-TOE SNAP."

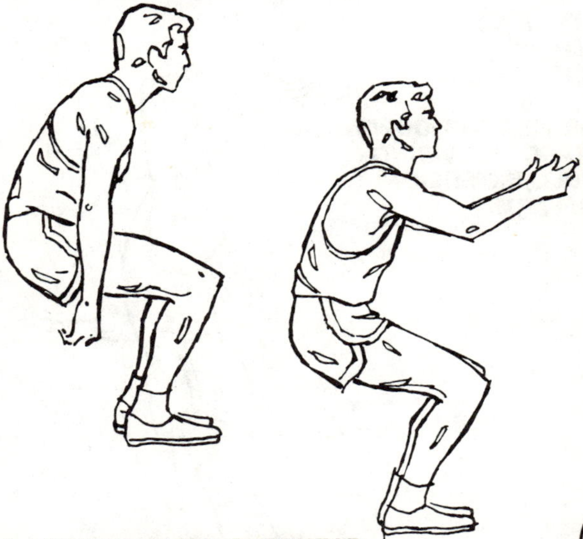

4. THRUST ARMS OVERHEAD TO ACHIEVE GREATER HEIGHT.

5. WHILE EXTENDING UPWARD, COCK ARM TO SWING AT BALL. POINT NONSTRIKING HAND AT BALL.

Arm Action

At the culmination of the upward arm swing, the striking arm is cocked behind the head while the nonstriking arm should aim at the oncoming volleyball. The back and legs also may be cocked in this position but they do not necessarily have to be so.

The spiking action begins as the nonstriking arm and the legs drive downward allowing full extension of the striking arm. The spiking hand is open to strike the ball. Lead the swing of the attacking arm with the elbow. The body usually "pikes" slightly as it approaches contact position. The final power is driven to the ball by a rapid snap of the upper arm from the elbow.

A good spiker has both power and control, and is capable of a variety of shots up to the very last instant before contact with the ball.

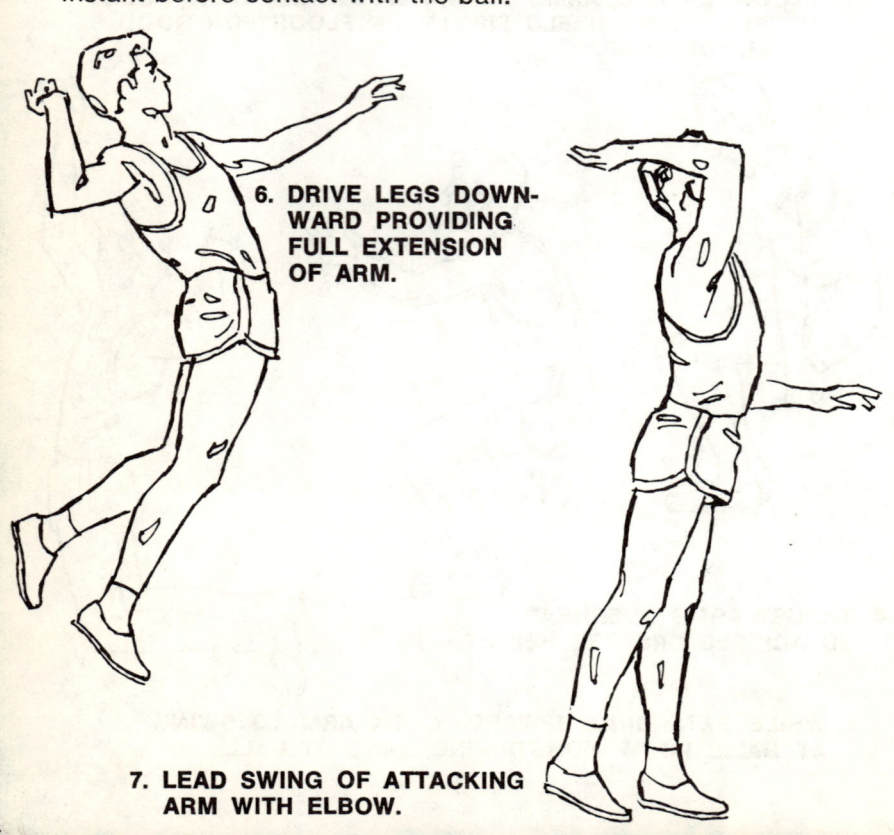

6. DRIVE LEGS DOWNWARD PROVIDING FULL EXTENSION OF ARM.

7. LEAD SWING OF ATTACKING ARM WITH ELBOW.

Ball Contact

Contact with the ball is made with the heel of an open hand. Some spikers keep their fingers spread for greater control while others use a tightly cupped hand for greater power.

At contact snap the wrist forcefully putting top spin on the ball, an action which provides greater control over the direction of the ball's flight. The higher and closer to the net that contact is made, the more the ball may be hit on top from in front of the body to give it a downward flight. The lower and farther away from the net that contact is made, the more underneath the ball should be hit to impart top spin. At contact or immediately thereafter, a vertical "plane of force" may often be drawn between the hand contacting the ball, the center of gravity and the "opposite" leg. In other words, the right arm, center of gravity and left leg are in a somewhat vertical plane at contact.

8. CONTACT BALL WITH HEEL OF OPEN HAND.

9. SNAP WRISTS PUTTING TOP SPIN ON BALL.

Follow Through

The *follow through* must not carry the spiker into the net, nor must his jump carry him under the net. The landing is cushioned by action of the feet and knees ultimately to achieve a *ready position* for the next play.

10. FOLLOW THROUGH TO TARGET.

11. CUSHION LANDING WITH FLEXING ACTION OF KNEES AND ANKLES.
    DO NOT TOUCH NET OR LAND UNDERNEATH.

the block

The *block* may be executed by one or more players. Blocking technique may vary depending upon size and jumping ability of the blocker and upon the rules.

Note: The International Volleyball Federation in 1964 and the United States Volleyball Association in 1967 adopted an "over-the-net" blocking rule.

The Defensive Block

The *defensive block* is employed to prevent a spiker from "killing" the ball. It is hoped that the ball will remain in play on the defensive side of the net to be set up as an offensive play.

Do not set up more than three feet from the net in anticipation of the attack. Raise hands to about shoulder height with elbows tucked in. As the ball is set, watch carefully to see where the spiker positions himself so as to intercept at the most probable spot or screen out a portion of the court, freeing teammates from that particular area.

Shuffle sideways rather than use crossover steps.

With a two-foot takeoff, the arms are kept close to the body and given a hard thrust upward. Elbows are straight but not locked and arms slope slightly forward. The hands are close to the plane of the net.

Spread the fingers slightly with the thumbs almost touching.

1. SET UP ABOUT THREE FEET FROM NET.
2. RAISE ARMS TO SHOULDER HEIGHT. POSITION BODY IN FRONT OF BALL.

Time the block as the ball crosses the net and contact ball before it starts to descend. Recover quickly and set up for an offensive play.

3. KEEP ARMS CLOSE TO BODY AND USE TWO-FOOT TAKEOFF TO THRUST UPWARD.

4. SPREAD FINGERS SLIGHTLY WITH THUMBS ALMOST TOUCHING. COCK WRISTS BACK.

5. TIME BLOCK AS BALL CROSSES NET AND MAKE CONTACT BEFORE BALL STARTS TO DESCEND.

The Offensive Block

The *offensive block* or *over-the-net block* is perhaps the most important offensive weapon in International Volleyball. The aim of the offensive block is to "kill" the ball rather than keep it in play.

The initial approach is similar to that of the defensive block only that the wrists need not be cocked to as great an extent.

As the ball leaves the setter's hands, assess where the ball will come down. Until the point of contact, there is little reason to watch the ball. Focus your entire attention on the spiker.

With the spiker and you in the air, the game is as intricate and fast as a boxing match. You must compensate for the spiker's every move.

The jump to block is executed slightly earlier than in the case of the defensive block. Contact should be made two to three inches on the opponent's side of the net.

1. AS BALL LEAVES SETTER'S HANDS, ADJUST TO WHERE BALL WILL COME DOWN.

2. SOON AS POSSIBLE, FOCUS ATTENTION ON SPIKER, NOT ON BALL.

With good wrist action, snap the ball hard to the floor. Recover quickly, not allowing wrists or arms to touch the net.

3. JUMP STRAIGHT UP, SLIGHTLY EARLIER THAN FOR DEFENSIVE BLOCK.

4. DO NOT DRIFT SIDEWAYS ON JUMP. AS SPIKER CONTACTS BALL, MOVE HANDS CLOSE TO PLANE OF NET.

5. CONTACT BALL TWO TO THREE INCHES ON OPPONENT'S SIDE OF NET.

6. SNAP BALL TO FLOOR WITH GOOD WRIST ACTION. DO NOT TOUCH NET.

the Japanese roll

Perhaps one of the most popular athletic teams in the world's history of athletics was the 1964 Japanese Women's Olympic Volleyball Team. This dedicated group of athletes trained fanatically for a number of years to win the Gold Medal in women's volleyball. Stories of their savage training and their victories saturated the world's news media. They won their Olympic championship without loss of a single match.

Their most dramatic impact on the volleyball in North America came in our adoption of their style of diving and recovery of shots which were previously considered to be unplayable. Although other teams had previously used this technique, the Japanese popularized it in the United States, hence the name, the *Japanese Roll*.

Japanese Roll Techniques

The *one-hand dig* coupled with the *Japanese Roll* is the most common method for the defensive player to get maximum court coverage. Of course when possible, it is desirable to play the ball defensively utilizing the forearm pass. When the ball is out of reach for this type of pass, the defensive player must maximize body extension with a one-hand dig for the ball, then quickly return to a ready position without injury.

Assume a ready position with the body low to the floor. Hands and arms are held in position as for a "forearm" pass.

Extend body fully toward the ball while keeping the center of gravity low to the ground. Contact ball on the lower portion of the forearm.

Usually, first contact with the floor is with the side of the leg or buttocks.

Tuck the body and roll over the back to return to an upright, ready position. Going to the right, the roll sequence is right buttock, across the back and over the opposite shoulder.

To the left, the sequence is left buttock, across the back and over the opposite shoulder.

1. **READY POSITION**
   Body Low to Floor. Hands and Arms in Position for Forearm Pass. Head up.

2. **KEEP CENTER OF GRAVITY LOW.**

3. EXTEND BODY FULLY TO REACH BALL. CONTACT BALL ON LOWER FOREARM. WATCH BALL CLOSELY. SWING AND FOLLOW THROUGH, PLACING BODY IN POSITION FOR ROLL.

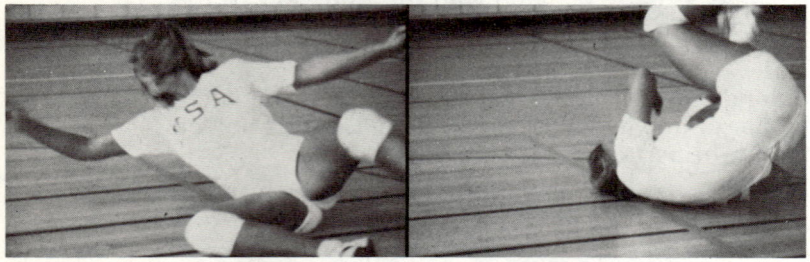

4. TUCK BODY AND ROLL ACROSS BACK.

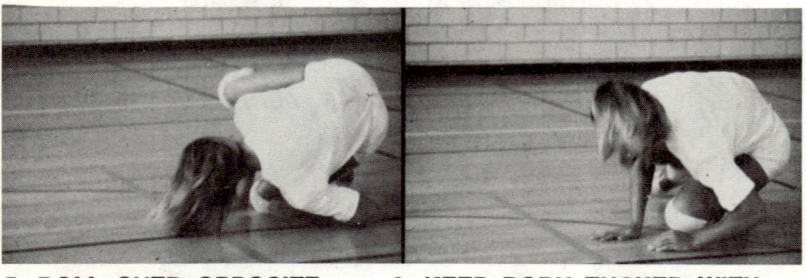

5. ROLL OVER OPPOSITE SHOULDER.

6. KEEP BODY TUCKED WITH HANDS AND FEET ON FLOOR.

7. RETURN TO READY POSITION.

Diagram of Court

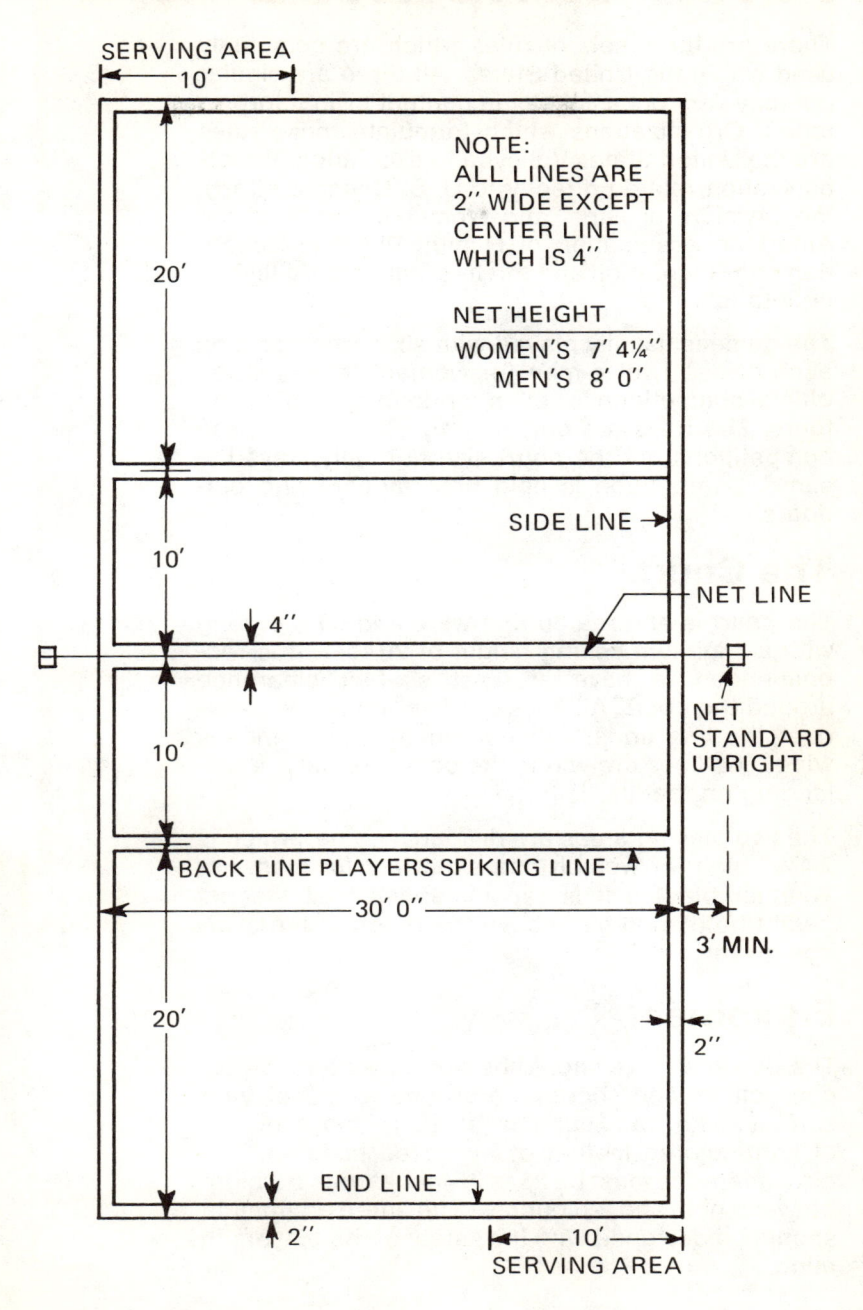

rules simplified

There are three sets of rules which are commonly used within the United States. All three are similar but may vary occasionally in content or in interpretation. Organizations which formulate these rules are the United States Volleyball Association (the organization related directly to U. S. Olympic effort), the Division for Girls' and Women's Sports of the American Association of Health, Physical Education and Recreation and the International Volleyball Federation.

The game is usually played with six participants on each of two twelve-man (or woman) teams. Often official competition is set up for doubles, triples and fours. The rules are only slightly altered for these competitions but the court size normally stays the same. Competition is held both indoors and outdoors.

The Court

The court is an area 30 feet wide and 60 feet long with a minimum ceiling height of 26 feet. It is recommended to have at least six-feet clearance around the court. All lines are two inches wide except the line under the net which is four inches wide. The lines are within the court area and a ball landing on the line is good.

The two playing areas are divided by a net which is 7'4¼" high for women and eight feet for men. For younger players it is recommended that the net height be placed just above the reach of the average player.

Equipment

The player's attire should be appropriate for vigorous activity and shoes appropriate to the playing surface. The ball must be of 12 or more pieces of light-colored leather or approved material. The circumference must be 25 to 27 inches with a weight between nine and ten ounces. The entire equipment should be designed with the safety of the players in mind.

The Game

To win a game, a team must score 15 points and be ahead by at least two points. If the score reaches 14-14, play continues until the winner achieves a two-point advantage. However, it is sometimes necessary to use time limits or other maximum scores to determine the winner.

The game begins with the service. If the serving team wins the play, a *point* is scored for the serving team. If the receiving team wins the play, a *side-out* is scored. The team which scored the side-out then rotates players clockwise and the player moving to **position number 1** becomes the server. Serves must be made from the service area behind the court.

(NOTE: Diagrams begin on following page.)

Each team is allowed three legal contacts with the ball before it must be returned to the opponent's court. No players may ordinarily contact the ball twice consecutively.

The Normal Sequence of Plays Will Be:
1. A pass by the serve receiver or defensive player.
2. A set to an appropriate front court player.
3. An attack by a front court player.

At times the first play will be a block if the opponents are attacking the ball. Only players in the front court **(Positions 2, 3 and 4)** may attack or block. Blocks may reach over the net but may not touch the ball before the attack is made. Spikers may only cross the net on the follow through. It is illegal to touch the net. Backcourt players **(Positions 1, 5 and 6)** may only attack from behind the back line player's spiking line which is ten feet from the net.

A team is allowed two 30-second time outs per game. Substitutions are somewhat limited depending upon the rules. Players must be in proper rotational order during the serve, but are free to change positions after the serve.

A match will be either two of three or three of five games.

The interpretation of a legally hit ball is in constant flux. In general, double hits are illegal; but the current trends are to allow more liberal ball handling and "soft spiking."

Team Tactics

The game of power volleyball has many complex tactics. These tactics fall into these general categories: **the serve, the serve reception, the offense and the defense.** The most fundamental of each is presented here.

Court Positions

The court is commonly divided into six positions. **(Fig. 1)**

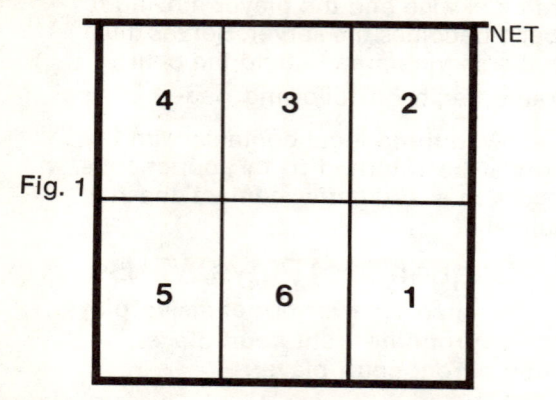

			NET
4	3	2	
5	6	1	

Fig. 1

Players

At the start of a game, the six players must assume a certain rotational order which is similar to the court positions. Note that the players will rotate clockwise during the game through the court positions. **(Fig. 2).**

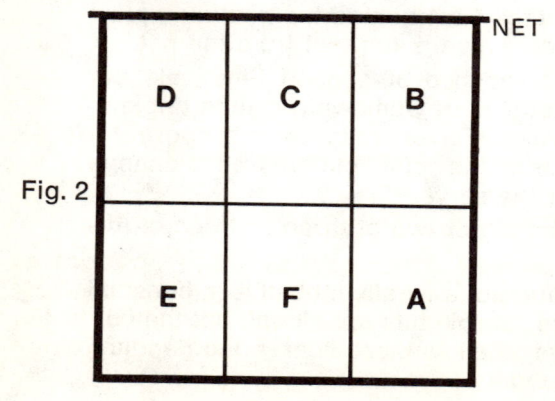

			NET
D	C	B	
E	F	A	

Fig. 2

Functions of Players

The most commonly used offensive system in the United States is called **the 4-2.** In this system there will be two players designated as setters ○ . These two setters will be lined up opposite to each other in the rotational order. In **figure 3** players A and D have arbitrarily been selected as setters.

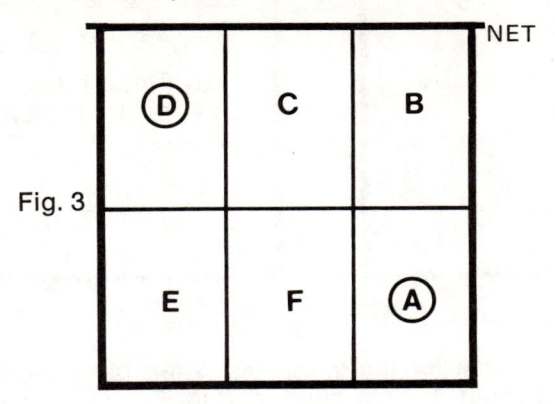

Fig. 3

There are also four players designated as spikers or attackers △ . **(Fig. 4)**

Fig. 4

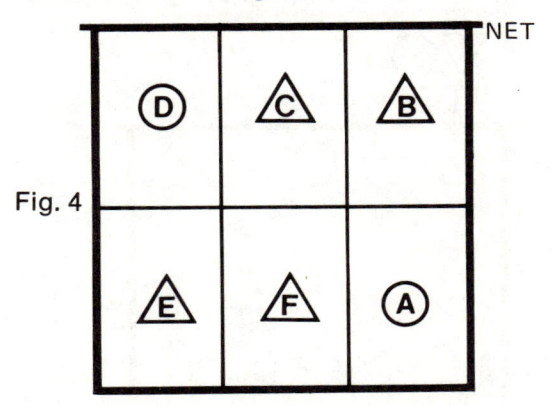

The Offensive System

The **4 spiker-2 setter offense** either positions or moves the front court setter in the center of the front offensive line. This system with the setter in the center and the spikers on each sideline has three major advantages:

1. An attack from the side of the court allows the attacker 42 feet diagonally across the court into which he may hit the ball. **(Fig. 5)**

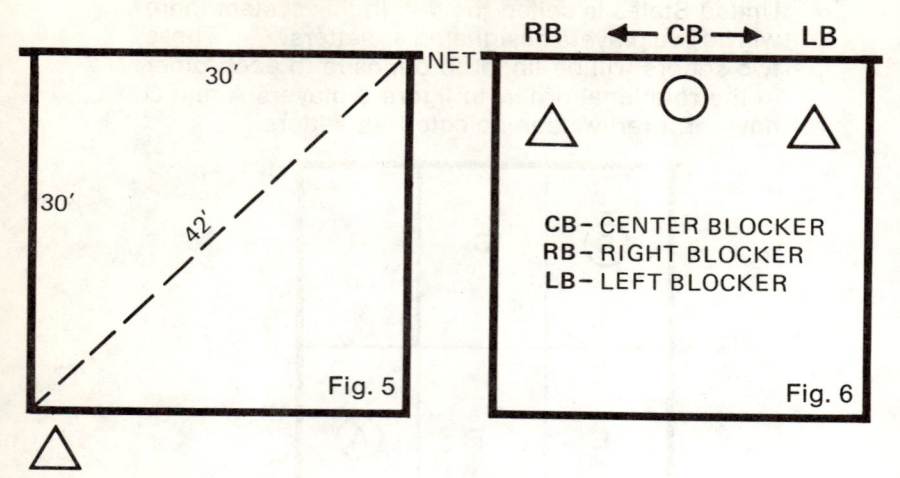

Fig. 5

Fig. 6

CB – CENTER BLOCKER
RB – RIGHT BLOCKER
LB – LEFT BLOCKER

2. It is difficult for the opposing center blocker to cover adequately both spikers. **(Fig. 6)**

3. An attack from the corner is often blocked out of bounds by the opponents. **(Fig. 7)**

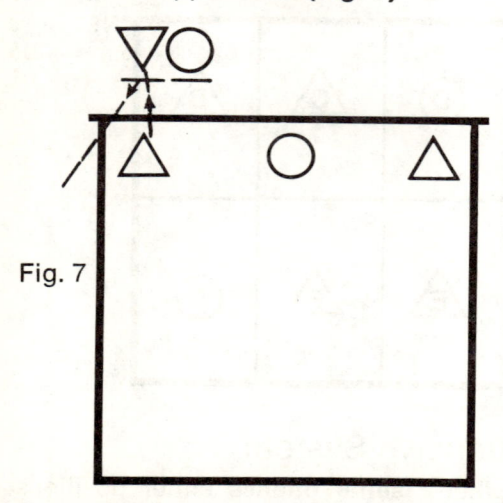

Fig. 7

The Serve Reception Patterns

The common serve reception pattern has five players in position to pass the ball while the setter removes himself from the pattern. This pattern is often called **the "W."** The pattern requires the front two attackers to position themselves in the wide front positions and the back players **(Nos. 1, 5, 6)** to be in the inner and back positions □.

In **figure 8** note that the setter has been eliminated from the receiving pattern since his position has no effect on the shape of the formation. Later in **figures 11, 12 and 13** the setter will be front left, center front and front right respectively.

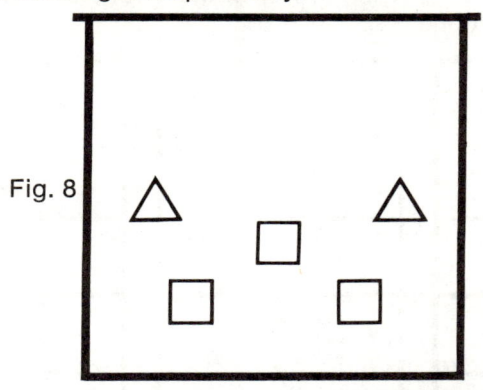

Fig. 8

The Serve Receiving Responsibilities

Figure 9 approximates the areas of responsibility for each player in the receiving pattern. The front spikers **must pass** most of the short serves while the deep players **must call** for the balls to inform teammates of their intentions. The various lines may

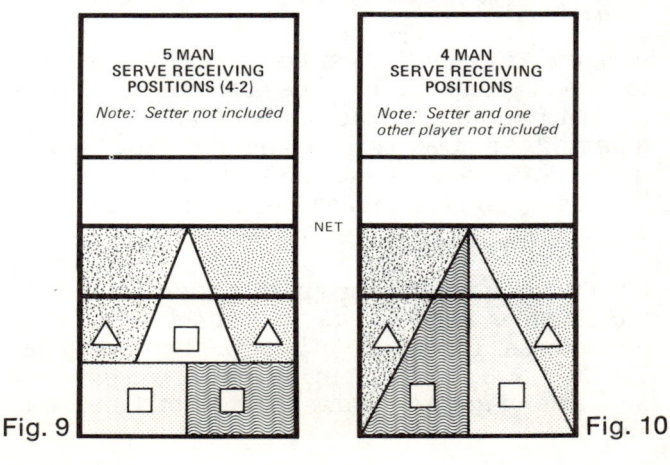

Fig. 9

5 MAN
SERVE RECEIVING
POSITIONS (4-2)

Note: Setter not included

NET

4 MAN
SERVE RECEIVING
POSITIONS

Note: Setter and one other player not included

Fig. 10

move up or back to anticipate the type of serve which must be passed. At times a team may choose to receive with only four players in the passing pattern. **Figure 10** gives the responsibilities of the four man pattern.

The Serve Reception Positions

Diagrams 11, 12 and 13 show the exact positions of specific players. The patterns show the setter successively in the left front, center front and right front positions.

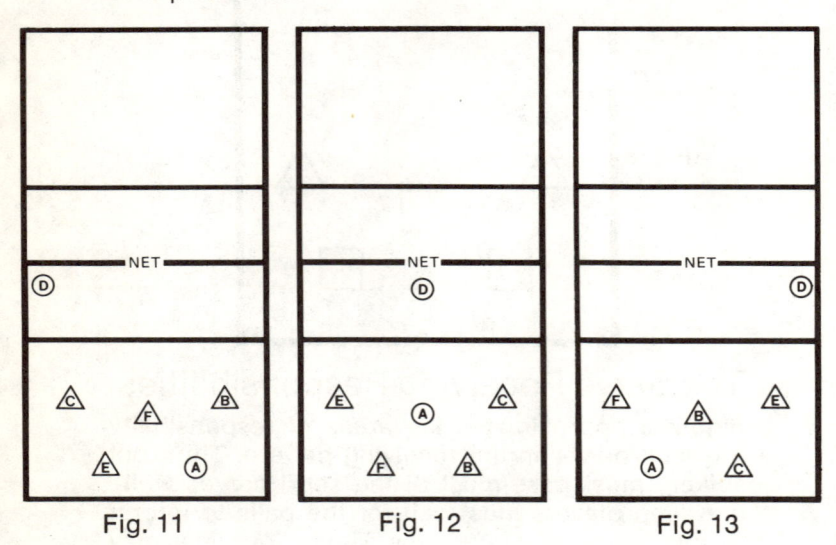

Fig. 11   Fig. 12   Fig. 13

Overlap

In **figure 11** setter D must be cautioned to remain to the left of spiker C until the ball is served. Player C must also be closer to the net than player F. In **figure 12**, few overlap problems are experienced. In **figure 13**, setter D must be to the right of spiker E and E must also be closer to the net than B.

Offensive Variety

Most teams attempt to establish a normal attack on the sidelines but then vary the attack to surprise the defense. The variety of sets will be the **regular (0), the 1, 2, 3** and **4**. All but the regular will be lower and faster. **Figure 14** shows the arcs of the various sets.

Basic defensive ready position is diagrammed in **figure 15.**

Fig. 14

Defensive Systems

There are two defensive patterns in common use in the United States today. Each one has many minor varieties. As the offensive patterns have numbers to designate them, the defensive patterns are usually given colors to distinguish them.

NOTE: Line (—) over symbol denotes "blockers."

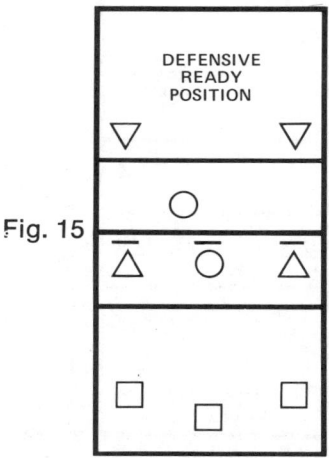

Fig. 15

DEFENSIVE READY POSITION

The White Defensive Pattern

This pattern is used most by men's teams and by more highly skilled women's teams. In it, the center back defensive player remains deep in the court and the blockers attempt to protect the sideline. **(Fig. 16)**

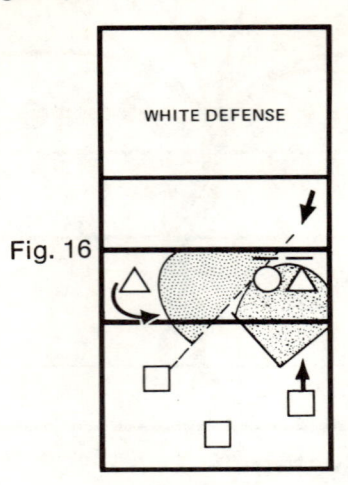

Fig. 16

WHITE DEFENSE

The Red Defensive Pattern

This pattern is found most commonly in women's competition or with men who are defending against the dink. The blockers must now protect more of the cross court attacks. **(Fig. 17)**

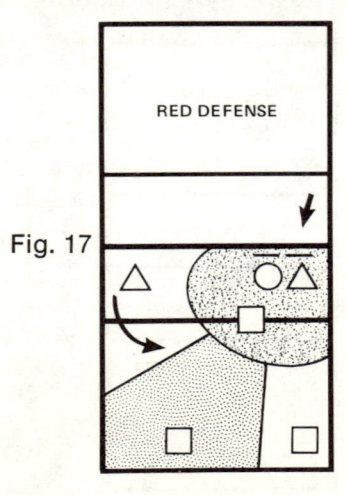

Fig. 17

RED DEFENSE

glossary of power volleyball terms:

ATTACK: The act of jumping into the air to hit the ball from above the level of the net into the opponent's court.

BLOCK: A defensive play by one or more players who attempt to intercept the ball as it passes over the net. In power volleyball it is legal for the blockers to reach over the net to block the ball as soon as the attack is made.

DEFENSE: The action by a team when the ball is controlled by its opponents. Defense is primarily a matter of team tactics. However, there are certain individual techniques which attempt to convert the defense to the offense. These include the **block, the dig, the dive** and **the roll.** (Some authorities consider **the serve reception** in this category.)

DIG: Recovery of an opponent's attack made by playing the ball with one or two hands or arms.

DINK: An attack in which the ball is hit with little force from the fingertips or fist. There are many interpretations as to the legality of the various techniques for the dink.

DIVE: A defensive technique employed to increase the forward range of motion. The defensive player dives forward, recovers a difficult shot then lands upon his chest and abdomen after being cushioned by his hands and arms.

FOREARM PASS: A ball played in an underhand manner. The forearms, held away from the body, act as a surface from which the pass can be made.

FOUL: An encroachment of the rules or a failure to play the ball properly as permitted under the rules.

GAME: To win a game, a team must score 15 points and be ahead by at least two points. If the score reaches 14-14, play continues until the winner achieves a two-point advantage. However, it is sometimes necessary to use time limits or other maximum scores to determine the winner.

OFFENSE: The action by the team controlling the ball. Offensive techniques include **the serve, the serve reception, the set** and **the attack.**

OVERHAND OR FACE PASS: A ball played from in front of the face with the fingertips of both hands. The hands must be in such a position that the passer is able to see the back of his hands.

OVERLAP: A foul committed as players stand in incorrect rotational order before the ball is served. When referring to **figure 2,** no player may infringe on the territory of a player immediately adjacent to him. For instance, **player F** has only three players immediately adjacent to him. He must remain behind **player C** and in between **players E and A.** In the patterns of power volleyball, the interpretations of overlap become relatively complex.

PASS: The controlled movement of the ball usually from one player to another on the same team. It may be either a forearm pass or an overhand pass. Usually this term is applied to the first play of the ball after it has crossed the net and often is applied only to the serve reception.

PLAY-OVER: A play-over is the act of putting the ball into play again without awarding a point or a side-out.

POINT: A point is awarded to the serving team only when the receiving team commits a foul.

POWER VOLLEYBALL: A game distinguished from recreational volleyball by the amount of organization needed for highly refined implementation of team strategy and individual skills. It is a game for players who possess a certain amount of quickness, alertness, coordination and stamina, and who desire to further develop the same.

ROLL: A defensive technique employed to increase the sideward range of motion. The defensive player lunges sideward, recovers a difficult shot then rolls over the back and shoulder to regain a defensive position.

SERVE: The technique in which the ball is put into play. Serves may be classified in many ways. If classified by arm swing, they are **the underhand, overhand** and **roundhouse serves.** If classified by ball movement, they are **spin serves** and **floating serves.** Most power volleyball players use some form of the floating serve.

SET: A pass, made overhand or underhand, hit into the air for the purpose of placing the ball in position for the attack. Normally the set is the second hit by the offensive team.

SIDE-OUT: Side-out shall be declared and the ball given to the opponents to serve when the serving team commits a foul. Points are not scored on a side-out.

SOFT SPIKE: An attack in which the ball is hit at less than maximum force to gain some tactical advantage.

SPIKE: An attack in which the ball is hit with a great force.

notes